What every intranet team should know
written by James Robertson

ISBN: 978-0-9808131-1-1

Published by
Step Two Designs

www.steptwo.com.au
contact@steptwo.com.au

PO Box 551, Broadway NSW 2007, Australia
Phone: +61 2 9319 7901

Introduction

Hidden from outside view, intranet best practices are not easy to discover. It comes as a surprise to many teams to discover that their challenges are not unique, and that the issues they are wrestling with are the same as those encountered the world over.

In the decade and more that Step Two has been working on intranets, we have seen a huge number of sites, and have talked with countless intranet teams. Our knowledge of intranets encompasses Australia and New Zealand, South-East Asia, Europe and the US.

Across all these continents, we see the importance of intranets, and the pivotal role that they play within organisations. No-one would now consider the possibility of turning their intranets off; some even use a day's unplanned downtime to demonstrate how much their intranets are needed.

Yet despite the growth of intranets, they have yet to fully deliver the business benefits that are desired by all. We hear the same story from many intranet teams: insufficient resources, little senior management recognition, constraining technology, and challenges in keeping content up to date.

It need not be this way. As we have learned about intranets, we have seen a number of fundamental concepts and approaches emerge that can guide intranet teams to greater success. We have captured the most important of these ideas in this book, to act as a guide for intranet teams and the organisations they serve.

This is, quite deliberately, a slim volume. We have written literally thousands of pages on intranets, but few have time to read a phone book's worth of text. So we have distilled our knowledge to a few key concepts, to get you kick-started on the journey to a remarkable intranet.

Table of contents

Six phases of
intranet
evolution

Intranets are surprisingly alike the world over. Regardless of whether they have been developed in Europe, the US or Australia, they share similar characteristics and histories.

This is not to say that they are identical, or that they should strive to be so. While the best intranets reflect the organisations they serve, intranet teams are all confronted with similar challenges and issues.

Public sector agencies, for-profit companies, non-profits, large and small organisations all raise common topics when brought together at conferences and workshops.

These issues and needs arise from the shared history of intranets, and their common evolution. From their earliest days, intranets go through similar stages and growing pains, and these evolutionary stages strongly influence the current sites, and explain their strengths and weaknesses.

It is vital that intranet teams understand this evolution, as it explains the states of their current sites. The history of intranets also allows teams to identify where to go next, and what improvements to make.

Understanding the evolution of intranets helps teams to avoid common pitfalls and dead ends. Intranets can be guided confidently forward, delivering greater benefits for staff and their organisations at every new stage.

Some years back we outlined our 'six phases of intranet evolution', and this remains a clear description of the history of intranets. We share the six phases here, and hope that these will strike a chord with all intranet teams.

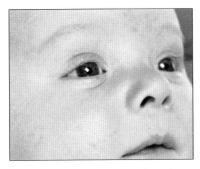

Phase 1: the intranet is born!

Phase 2: rapid organic growth

Phase 3: repeated redesigns

Phase 4: intranet usability

Phase 5: useful, not just usable

Phase 6: business tool

Phase 1: the intranet is born!

In the beginning, the intranet is born. At the outset, this is often the product of a single individual who sees the potential value of the intranet, or has become excited by intranets seen in other organisations.

This initial intranet will be very small, and may only address one specific area or topic, such as:

- IT intranet

- HR intranet

- call centre intranet

- policies & procedures site

Depending on when the site was created, it may be published using very simple tools or even produced by hand-coding HTML. It will almost certainly be maintained centrally at the outset, guided by the vision of the original creator.

Whatever the scope or purpose of the original intranet, it's enough to demonstrate the potential value of the site, and to generate further interest throughout the organisation.

Very quickly the intranet starts to proliferate, and we enter into phase 2, rapid organic growth.

> Many organisations have now had intranets for 10–15 years, and a lot has changed in that time. Intranets were often started as a hobby, created in FrontPage, with blink text, animated gifs, scrolling banners and bright colours. These days are thankfully long gone, replaced by professional management of intranets and clean modern designs (to a large extent at least!).

Phase 2: rapid organic growth

Once interest in the intranet has been sparked, it grows rapidly. Many more authors start to publish content, drawn from business units across the organisation, leading to a proliferation of new pages.

This phase of growth will typically last years, and the intranet ends up consisting of thousand or tens of thousands of pages (we know of major corporations that have intranets with millions of pages!).

These pages will be scattered across a single site, dozens of sites, or hundreds of separate intranet sites loosely joined together. Content as far as the eye can see.

The key characteristic of this phase is that the growth is organic. There is no overall plan, strategy, governance or direction. Information is published for one of two reasons:

1. In the hope that it will be useful to someone, somewhere at some point. (This is the source of 80% of content.)

2. For vanity reasons, showcasing a business unit and its services. (This typically accounts for 20% of content.)

In the absence of an overall strategy or a true understanding of staff needs, some information hits its target, while other content falls well short.

In an early workshop, one participant described their intranet as having 'grown like coral'. We liked this as a good metaphor for organic growth: no overall plan, many different colours and shapes, but attractive and productive nonetheless. Some time later, however, a workshop participant said 'no, that's not my intranet, mine has grown like a fungus'. Still organic growth, but not quite so attractive!

A common reaction to the results of organic growth

Organic, unmanaged growth inevitably generates problems seen across many intranets, including:

- out of date, incomplete or poorly written content

- inconsistent, sometimes competing designs

- ineffective overall structure for the site

- search that works poorly (or hasn't been implemented at all)

- staff find the intranet frustrating and hard to navigate

- ad hoc publishing processes

- unclear or non-existent content ownership

- no content management system (or similar publishing tool)

What every intranet team should know

- poor governance and site management

- low status and under-resourced intranet team

- little visibility of the intranet at senior management levels

- and, when a check is done, very few staff actually use the site (or at least, are not using it anywhere near as much as they should)

Does this strike a chord? Every intranet has gone through this phase, as an inevitable consequence of the site's organic growth.

In the face of these growing problems, the intranet team (or intranet individual) is horrified. How did the site get into this state! The inevitable reaction is to trigger a redesign.

Phase 3: repeated redesigns

The intranet is broken, inconsistent, poor quality and hard to use. The intranet team (or individual) lock themselves in a room for a few weeks or months, surrounded by printouts of the intranet, sitemaps, and plenty of paper.

The goal is to create a new 'more logical' intranet, with a consistent top-level structure and standard page designs. All the existing pages are then squeezed somewhere into the new design, with as much content reviewed as time allows.

A range of supporting changes are also made during the redesign:

- an overall rebranding of the site, including new page designs

- potentially a new name (via a naming competition?)

- changes to the design or functionality of the home page

At then end of this project, the new site is launched and heavily promoted: 'roll up, roll up, have a look at the redesigned and consistent site, you'll love it!'.

Promotional activities may include:

- mousemats, stress balls or helium balloons

- posters on walls and next to the lifts

- brochures and other educational material

- t-shirts and caps

- launch party and lunch-time instructional sessions

Briefly, all is well. There is a spike in usage following the promotion of the new site, but this settles back down fairly quickly to levels typical of the old site.

Over time, new content is added, and consistency starts to unravel. Additional sites are launched, and the challenge remains to keep the current content up to date. Publishing processes are still ad hoc, and senior visibility remains low. Resources and budget for the intranet (and the intranet team) remain tight.

Fast forward three years, and the intranet has slid back down into disrepair. Despite the significant work involved in the redesign, the intranet is wrestling with many of the same challenges seen in phase 2, the era of rapid organic growth.

The intranet team despairs, how did the site get back into this mess! 'Let's do another redesign, we'll get it right for sure this time.'

This is why this is the phase of repeated redesigns. Every two or three years, the intranet is reworked (to a lesser or greater extent), but the site continues to struggle with the same underlying challenges.

Repeated redesigns: while the intranet has been cosmetically improved, it remains a pig.

In an organisation that has had an intranet for over a decade, there may be three, four or five redesigns. The site looks more modern, but it is not substantially different. The intranet contains the same content and provides the same functionality, but has just been reshuffled.

The fundamental problem with these redesigns is that they don't address the underlying issues with the site. These include the lack of governance and effective publishing processes, and the poor resources devoted to the site.

This can be summed up as 'lipstick on a pig'. The site may be cosmetically more attractive, but it's still a pig. So, how do we escape this cycle of repeated redesigns?

Phase 4: intranet usability

There is one other major problem with the redesigns conducted in phase 3: how the structure of the new site is determined. Locked in a room, the intranet team worked hard to identify a sensible and consistent structure for the site.

Unfortunately, what made sense to the intranet team (as the designers) does not necessarily makes sense to staff in the rest of the organisation. Logical structure, when laid out on a huge sitemap, does not necessarily work well when users navigate page-by-page through the site, relying on the links they are provided with at each point.

In phase 4, end users (staff) are brought into the design process, and are directly involved in testing and refining the designs. In this phase, the intranet team starts to make use of a range of 'user-centred design' (UCD) techniques.

These include techniques drawn from the fields of usability, including paper prototyping and usability testing. Information architecture techniques such as card sorting are also used.

Together, these provide a structured methodology for developing an intranet (or any other site) that ensures that it is easy to use.

These techniques help the intranet team go beyond the opinions of stakeholders, users and senior management. Instead, they are able to conduct realistic tests with staff to ensure that common tasks can be completed quickly and confidently on the redeveloped site.

> A whole section, starting on page 54, has been devoted to how to design an intranet, including coverage of user-centred design techniques and fundamental design principles.

What every intranet team should know

During this phase, many other intranet issues are addressed, marking a move towards more professional management of the site. These include:

- improving or replacing the search engine

- implementing or replacing the content management system

- establishing basic intranet policies and governance

- formalising authoring and publishing responsibilities

- formalising the role of the intranet team

- communicating the use and value of the intranet more widely

- presenting a business case to senior management (even if in a preliminary form)

This is a large piece of work, at least 12–24 months in length. It does, however, deliver a site that is easy to use, while addressing many of the behind-the-scenes issues that impact intranets.

The intranet team, while exhausted, is pleased to go out to the business to promote the new site, and the benefits it offers. A communication campaign is conducted, and interest is generated.

And yet this is still not enough for intranets to truly succeed.

Phase 5: useful, not just usable

In phase 5, the intranet team recognises that there is a world of difference between usable and useful. Following best-practice user-centred design techniques, phase 4 can deliver a site that is very easy to use. Information can be quickly and easily found on the site, and search works well. Despite this, the site can be entirely useless.

All too often, the redesigns of the site focus on the content that is currently on the site. Where did this come from? It came from phase 2, the era of rapid organic growth, when content was published in the hope that it would be useful, or for vanity reasons.

At what point did anyone check whether this was the information that staff really needed? Did the team take time to find out whether there is information and tools that staff need that has never been on the intranet? In the busy and tiring redesign project, there is often no chance to do either of these things.

The redesign shuffles around the existing site, making it easier to use, but not making it more useful. To address this, phase 5 starts to introduce a new set of techniques that go by variety of names: user research, requirements gathering, or needs analysis.

These provide a toolbox of structured techniques that allow staff needs to be discovered in detail, without asking the difficult question 'what do you want?'.

With these techniques, the intranet team uncovers in-depth information about staff needs, issues, roadblocks and opportunities. The intranet team is also able to understand the differences in needs between staff groups and locations.

This phase sees the intranet team deliver a site that is much more directly tied into the day-to-day activities of staff, and is more than just a dumping ground for second-hand content.

As the intranet grows in its value to staff, it starts to transform into a key business tool.

For more on the techniques that can be used to discover staff needs, see page 40.

Phase 6: intranet as a business tool

This is the intranet as the way of doing things, a site that supports the needs of operational staff throughout the organisation. Clear business benefits are delivered that are tied into broader corporate goals, such as customer service, product sales or staff efficiency.

The intranet also starts to go beyond being just a publishing platform for corporate policies, procedures and news. Instead, it integrates a much broader range of functionality, underpinned by a clear intranet strategy and roadmap.

Intranets in this phase have also built a clear business case, giving the intranet team enough resources to be effective. This is underpinned by clear governance, and the strong involvement of business units across the organisation.

These are the case studies that appear in magazines and online, and this is a future phase for most organisations. Even in large and well-resourced organisations, it is rare that the whole intranet has reached this level.

There is no shortcut to get to phase six, and intranets need to work through the underlying issues first to uncover their true value. It is also a moving target, not an end goal, and a clear sign of a successful intranet is that it is consistently improving.

Phase six offers an exciting glimpse of the future of intranets, and we'll explore what elements make up this business-centric intranet in the next chapter.

Six phases of intranet evolution

We have explored six phases of intranet evolution:

1. the intranet is born!

2. rapid organic growth

3. repeated redesigns

4. intranet usability

5. useful, not just usable

6. intranet as a business tool

Most intranets go through these phases, and they help to explain why intranets are the way they are. To a certain extent, intranets need to go through these evolutionary steps, growing in response to needs and then progressively formalising their management.

In practice, the picture will be more complex than this simple model. In any larger organisation, different corners of the intranet may be at different stages of evolution. Sites may also go backwards, perhaps being forced into another redesign as a result of changing the technology platform.

Organisations starting out on the intranet journey can learn from these phases of evolution. While organic growth is necessary, it can be managed in a way that avoids many of the problems experienced by older sites. Learning from the lessons of others, new intranets can also move much more quickly to the later stages of intranet evolution.

Most importantly, intranet teams of any size and history can use these phases of evolution to work out which step to take next, to help them deliver a site that is truly successful.

Where is your site at in the six phases of intranet evolution?

Assess your current state

The intranet is product of its history and evolution. Understand where your site sits along the six phases, and build a clearer understanding of its current strengths and weaknesses. Recognise that you are not alone in wrestling with these challenges, and consider benchmarking yourself against sites in other similar organisations.

Plan your next steps

Intranets deliver the most value when they progress through the stages of evolution. By knowing where the site is currently, you can plan the next round of improvements, whether it is to improve the usability of the site, or to research staff needs in greater detail.

Always work towards delivering a business-centric intranet, that becomes the 'way of doing things' throughout the organisation.

Four purposes of the intranet

Content

Communication

Collaboration

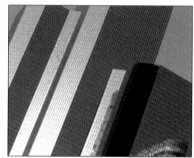

Activity

There are four fundamental purposes of an intranet: content, communication, collaboration, and activity. Each plays a key role in meeting staff and organisational needs, and successful intranets maintain a balance between all four purposes.

Intranet teams benefit from having a clear picture of the current focus of their intranets, highlighting areas of strength and weakness. By focusing on improving key areas, intranet teams can transform their intranets into valuable business tools.

1. Content

To this point, one of the primary purposes of intranets is to provide a repository for published information. This includes core corporate content, such as:

* human resources (HR)

* information technology (IT)

* finance

* travel

It also includes operational and business unit information, such as details on products and services, and frontline policies.

This is the intranet as a 'single point of entry' or a 'one stop shop' for corporate information. Pursuing this goal, sites can become very large, with tens of thousands of pages of content, and thousands of linked documents.

The challenge is to structure the site so that required information can be found among this huge mass of pages, as well as managing the content so it is trusted and up to date.

This is no easy task. Most intranets move towards a decentralised model of content publishing to support the creation and management of this broad cross-section of content. While this involves more staff in the publishing process, it brings its own challenges and issues.

There are a range of practical strategies and approaches that intranet teams can take to deliver great content. Skip ahead to page 68 to read more.

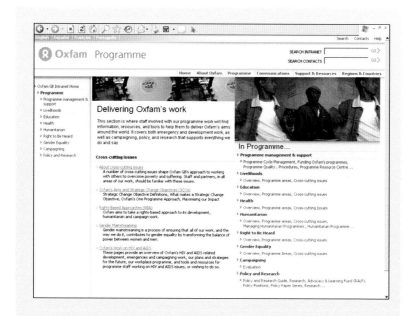

Oxfam UK uses their intranet to deliver support information for their key programmes of work

2. Communication

The intranet has a clear role to play as a corporate communication channel, one that reaches most staff across the organisation.

On most intranets, this consists of one or more news boxes on the home page. Regular items are published of organisation-wide interest, including major policy updates, senior management decisions, awards, and industry changes.

In most cases, there is a clear owner for intranet news: the internal communications team. They are responsible for publishing news, and often work to a daily publishing schedule.

Some of the intranet news items will be contributed by staff or individual business areas, while others will be sourced or written by the central intranet team. Many will be the product of major corporate campaigns, such as those relating to safety, HR, IT or culture.

While the intranet's role as a communications channel is well recognised, it only delivers on this objective when the site is being regularly used, and news alone is not enough to draw staff to the site. (If staff are only using the intranet once a week on average, they will miss a significant proportion of the published news.)

News can also be very high level, more related to corporate changes and organisational culture, than operational updates. When asked what kind of news they want, staff will routinely reply: 'the news that will impact my job'.

At present, intranets don't always do a great job of meeting this need. To achieve this, news needs to be directly related to key operational and frontline activities within organisations. The challenge is that this news will be tied to individual business areas, each needing different operational news.

This is a much greater volume of news than just a handful of items per week, overwhelming the simple news box on the home page. To address this, intranets are improving the robustness of news delivery, including finding ways of targeting news to specific audiences across the organisation.

Intranets therefore do a reasonable job of delivering news at present, but there is more work to be done, including establishing a stronger platform for operational news.

Innovative intranet communications

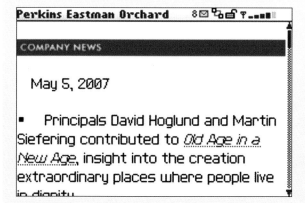

For Perkins Eastman, one of the largest architecture and design firms in the United States, the sharing and distribution of company, industry and staff news is a very important function. The screenshot above shows the news displayed on a BlackBerry, allowing them to reach architects when in the field or at client sites.

As new devices, such as the iPhone, are used more widely in organisations, it will become even easier to keep staff in touch with key news, regardless of where they are located.

At Swiss Post, there are some 10,000 postmen, parcel delivery staff and postbus drivers who do not have access to a computer while they work.

This is why Swiss Post created the 'Speaking Intranet News' that can be accessed using any phone and an 0800 toll free number. By dialling this number an computerised voice reads the latest news entries, providing field staff with a way of getting news even when on the road.

Both of these innovative examples show the intranet going beyond the desktop to deliver communications directly to staff, instead of just waiting for staff to visit the intranet.

3. Collaboration

Collaboration is a hot topic at present, fueled by the spread of wikis, blogs and team spaces through organisations. The growth of Share-Point is also bringing collaboration to the forefront of management thinking, and is providing intranets with a much richer toolbox of functionality.

Historically, there has been little corporate recognition of collaboration, and teams and business units were left with just email and shared network folders. Intranets acted solely as publishing and news platforms, providing access to corporate documents but not directly supporting collaboration.

The changing organisational landscape has made collaboration an imperative, to support knowledge sharing, enhance service delivery and improve competitiveness. The deployment of the latest generation of collaboration tools is therefore timely.

The challenge now is to place collaboration tools in the broader information landscape, and to expand them in a manageable way. For without caution, the unmanaged spread of collaboration tools will lead to greater fragmentation and confusion, making information harder to find not easier.

Collaboration tools also have the potential to compete with the intranet, providing a second home page for staff. Staff are left to wonder: 'Will I find this on the intranet? or in a wiki space? perhaps in that team's project space?'

A strategic approach to collaboration is required, to ensure that solutions meet local needs, while progressing broader corporate objectives for better information management.

Collaboration best practices are starting to become clear, and these include:

- establishing clear ownership and management of collaboration

- putting in place governance and support from the outset

- establishing an overall strategy that positions collaboration tools alongside other platforms

- developing a business case for collaboration that allows the necessary resources to be allocated

- designing collaboration tools for simplicity and ease of use

- giving access to collaboration tools from the intranet

- helping staff select the right tools and use them effectively

Ultimately, intranet teams cannot afford to ignore collaboration. The growth of these tools will continue and they can easily undermine the role of the intranet. Intranet teams are also ideally placed to manage collaboration, as they already have the right skills and focus.

The intranet should therefore encompass collaboration, placing it alongside the site's traditional publishing and communication role. This ensures that staff are able to quickly find the information they need, whether it's in one of the team spaces they have access to, or in the corporate sections of the site.

Step Two has published a best practice case study titled 'Governance and support for SharePoint team sites', and this provides a valuable example for all teams:

www.steptwo.com.au/products/teamsites

What every intranet team should know

Competitor Wiki

Scottrade is a privately-owned online brokerage based in St Louis, Missouri, with over 350 branches across 47 states. In a highly competitive industry, Scottrade needs to get its staff the information on competitor offerings they need to win business.

The Competitor Wiki has detailed information about the various trading platforms of each firm, along with information on the current promotions each firm is offering. Each wiki entry is also linked to the competitor's web site should further detail or explanation be needed when speaking with a current or prospective customer.

By giving frontline staff the ability to update content directly, publishing which previously took up to a month is done in an instant. They also have a channel to chat with each other and to share successful strategies.

With just a handful of pages, the competitor wiki directly targets a key need within Scottrade. Not just an example of a successful collaboration tool, but a remarkable business solution.

4. Activity

This is the intranet as a place for doing things, rather than just a place for reading things. Instead of just a policy on how to apply for leave, the intranet allows staff to actually apply for leave online, and have it processed quickly and transparently.

Let's use a simple example to demonstrate the point. Within any organisation there are literally hundreds of forms to be filled in, from stationery requests, to finance forms and IT security requests.

Traditionally, these were pieces of paper, stored in filing cabinets, or handed out by administrative staff. The intranet took a great leap forward, and replaced these paper forms with online forms, PDFs or Word documents on the site.

Now forms can be easily found in a single location. They are then downloaded, printed, filled in by hand, sent across by internal mail, typed back in, and then processed. If there is a problem with the form, such as a missing detail, a phone call is made to the applicant, or an email sent.

Not exactly a 21st century process! Instead of this, the intranet could provide actual web forms that can be filled in electronically. Pre-filling the staff member's details saves them time, and drop-down lists avoid mistakes. Even if the form just sends an email behind the scenes to the relevant area, this can be the start of implementing a more complete form solution, including back-end workflow for approval.

Of course, this is not just about forms, and there are hundreds of opportunities across any organisation, ranging from simple online applications to full business solutions. Administrative processes are a good target, as are key operational activities.

Meter reading application

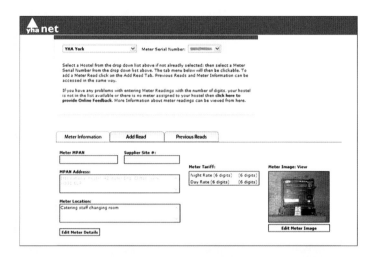

YHA operates a network of over 200 properties across England and Wales. As a member of Hostelling International, YHA is required to monitor and minimise energy consumption.

With a goal of reducing energy expenditure by 10% over two years, YHA established an online tool for collecting meter readings.

This greatly simplified meter reading for staff in hostels, and gave managers and head office staff the information they needed to manage and budget electricity.

The solution also made staff members' lives easier, eliminating the need to hunt around fruitlessly for electricity meters hidden in cupboards or in changing rooms, and replacing confusing paperwork.

This solution, not difficult to develop, was therefore a win for both staff and organisation. Integrated into the intranet, it also shows just one of the hundreds of opportunities for streamlining business processes that exist in every organisation.

Traditional role of intranets

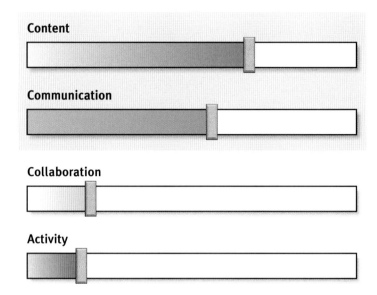

To this point, the primary focus of most intranets has been on content and communication. While these meet some organisational needs, they are not enough to ensure intranet success.

It is difficult to develop a business case for just content and communication, and any calculations of return on investment (ROI) are weak at best. The fundamental problem is that the intranet as a repository for corporate content and news is simply not tied directly enough into the daily working practices of staff.

When intranets focus solely on these two purposes, intranet teams will struggle to gain the resources and support they need to deliver the site they want. This is not to say that content and communication should be abandoned, but they do need to be part of a broader focus and strategy.

Delivering business value

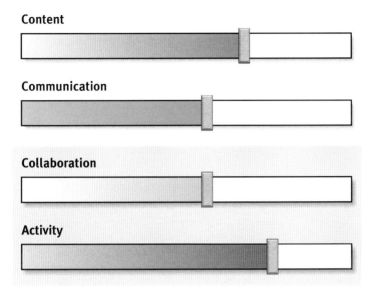

Content

Communication

Collaboration

Activity

Going forward, intranet teams need to focus on delivering business value, which will generate the support and resources required to grow and prosper. This will also help the intranet to gain recognition from senior management as a key business tool.

This involves pulling a greater focus on collaboration and activity, two areas historically neglected in most intranets. Of these, activity has the potential to deliver the clearest business benefits, by streamlining key processes, or simplifying activities.

Demonstrating ROI for activity is comparatively easy, particularly when the efficiency of existing practices is already being measured. Collaboration is also much more directly tied into daily work, and there is a clear case for supporting project delivery with better tools.

Get the balance right

Successful intranets find a balance between the four purposes, avoiding an excessive focus on one area and not neglecting any others. Each aspect has a role to play, supporting staff and the organisation as a whole.

Intranets need to play a broad role in the organisation, and teams should look for opportunities to add additional capabilities that benefit staff in their day-to-day work.

Over time, teams should steadily strengthen the intranet, maturing capabilities already delivered (such as news) and exploring the potential of activity and collaboration to streamline working practices.

Think of the model as a set of sliders that you can set to a mix that fits your organisation and culture. There is no one-size-fits-all focus for intranets, and the intranet team plays an important role in getting the balance right.

For example:

- The global intranet site of a multinational business may focus strongly on corporate content and global communications. Collaboration happens to a small degree between countries, but mostly within individual offices. Similarly, business solutions are developed at a country level, to match local laws and business needs.

- Within a manufacturing firm, the intranet is a vital repository for procedural and quality assurance information. Many of the business and operational systems are also accessed through the site, delivering considerable efficiency benefits. Collaboration and communication, however, are done face-to-face on the factory floor.

How well does your intranet address the four purposes?

Explore the role of intranets

There are four fundamental purposes of an intranet: content, communication, collaboration and activity (the intranet as a place for doing things). These define a broad role for intranets within organisations.

Focus on delivering business value

Intranet teams should steadily grow the intranet beyond just content and communication, to encompass activity and collaboration. This allows clear business benefits to be delivered, and helps staff to do their jobs more effectively.

Get the mix right

There is no single best approach to intranets, and strategies must match the organisation's needs and culture. Use the model as a 'mixer' to find the right balance between the four purposes.

How to find out what staff need

The intranet will be used if it is useful. In specific, it must be useful for actual staff, the expected users.

These are obvious statements to make, but much harder to achieve in practice. When teams are trapped in repeated redesigns (phase 3 of intranet evolution), they have a tendency to focus on the assumed needs of staff, or on 'core' content such as policies and procedures.

This is an opportunity for intranet teams to get out from behind their desks, and spend time in the field, talking (and listening) to staff across the business. The most time should be spent with operational and frontline staff (the staff who do the actual work).

Spending time in this way will generate many new ideas for intranet improvements. Equally importantly, it will renew the intranet team's enthusiasm for the site and their work, by putting a human face to intranet needs and issues.

In any larger organisation, however, this kind of research can be an overwhelming task. Of the thousands of staff, who to talk to? How to make sense of the sometimes competing priorities and needs?

A range of structured techniques can be used to uncover and understand staff needs in a practical and time-effective way. The techniques are known by many names: needs analysis, requirements gathering, user research, field research.

Regardless of what they are called, they provide a rich toolbox for understanding staff needs, frustrations, successes and roadblocks. Using these techniques helps to build a picture of the day-to-day operation of the organisation, and the environments that staff work in.

Once staff (and organisational) needs are understood, it becomes a relatively straightforward process to identify potential solutions.

Don't ask staff what they want!

To uncover staff needs, it seems sensible to ask questions such as:

- What is most useful on the intranet?

- What are the problems with the current intranet?

- What features are missing from the intranet?

- What additional information do you need?

- How else could the intranet help you with your job?

While they seem reasonable, these questions are almost entirely useless, as they require staff to have an understanding of intranets, and how they can support day-to-day work in organisations.

Staff have little understanding of intranets, because they don't need to. Instead, they have in-depth knowledge relating to their job role and activities, and it's the job of the intranet team to understand intranets.

Asking these types of questions generates one of two possible responses:

- 'I'm not sure. Can you give me some examples of how an intranet could help me?'

- 'I think it would be great if the intranet provided feature xyz!'

In the first case, staff are unable to provide meaningful input into intranet design or strategy. In the second, a wish list of features and tools is collected, but without ensuring that these ideas will actually be useful (or used) in practice.

Staff will also respond based on their current use of the intranet, which will reinforce existing practices, and make it harder (not easier) to build an innovative intranet.

Attempting to gain intranet ideas from staff in this way will not generate the hoped-for insights. There is, however, a better way.

Structured techniques

Intranet teams can easily uncover true staff needs without ever asking 'what do you want?'. Instead, as touched on earlier, there are a range of more structured ways for uncovering needs.

These techniques focus on what staff do in their jobs, what activities they are involved in, the information they require, and where they currently get it.

This allows staff to provide input on how they work, with the intranet team providing the expertise in intranet design, management and strategy.

By combining these together, many practical activities and improvements will be identified that will increase the usage of the intranet throughout the organisation.

A wide range of needs analysis techniques can be used, including:

1. surveys

2. focus groups and requirements workshops

3. staff interviews

4. stakeholder interviews

5. workplace observation

Together, these techniques will quickly build up a comprehensive picture of the organisation, and where the intranet can be of use. These techniques are also simple enough for all intranet teams to make use of them without requiring professional research skills.

Let's explore these techniques at a high level.

1. Surveys

Surveys are commonly used to gather the input of staff throughout an organisation, and their big advantage is their ability to generate a large number of responses.

Care must be taken when constructing survey questions. As much as possible, the questions should be specific, focusing on the recent experiences of the survey respondent, rather than on collecting broader opinions or perceptions about the site. The 'asking staff what they want' questions outlined earlier should also be avoided.

In practice, surveys are best suited to assessing the opinions of staff, rather than uncovering concrete needs. This makes surveys most suitable for:

- Measuring staff satisfaction. Intranet surveys conducted on a yearly basis are an effective way of gauging ongoing changes in staff satisfaction with the intranet. As before-and-after measurements, surveys can demonstrate the benefits from intranet redesigns.

- Gathering evidence for a business case. Widespread dissatisfaction with the current intranet can be used as a key element in the business case for an intranet redevelopment project. Be careful however: staff may be merely apathetic about the intranet instead of unhappy, which could undermine the business case.

In practice, surveys are less effective at obtaining the detailed, in-depth information needed to inform design and project planning decisions. For this reason, surveys should never be used as the sole mechanism to gather staff input, and must always be complemented with other techniques.

2. Focus groups and requirements workshops

These are facilitated discussions that focus on exploring a topic within a group setting. Widely used as a way of gathering input from larger numbers of staff, focus groups and requirements workshops are best used to explore current issues and problems, rather than to discuss wish lists of potential intranet ideas.

These sessions must be run carefully if they are to generate meaningful results. In particular, the group dynamics needs to be closely managed, to ensure that a small number of individuals do not dominate the sessions.

The same 'type' of staff should be involved in individual sessions. For example, staff from the call centre, hospital administrators, middle managers or HR staff. Multiple sessions are then run across the organisation to obtain a representative sample.

While focus groups and requirements workshops do allow a greater number of staff to be involved, they don't tend to uncover in-depth information about problems or needs. For this reason, they should always be used in conjunction with techniques such as staff interviews or workplace observation.

Art Center College Library
1700 Lida Street
Pasadena, CA 91103

3. Staff interviews

One-on-one interviews are a very effective way of gathering information on staff needs and issues. Held with a range of operational staff, these quickly build up a picture of key information needs.

When conducting interviews, avoid asking questions about the intranet itself. Instead, the interviews should explore how staff work, what this involves day-to-day, the information they need, and where they currently get it.

Good questions include:

- What is your job role?

- What are the main activities that make up your job?

- Who do you communicate most frequently with on work matters?

- Do you have policies or guidelines for your work?

- How do you get access to these?

- What information do you rely on during a normal working day?

- Where do you obtain this information?

- If you have a question, where do you go to find an answer?

- How do you find out about what's happening in the organisation?

Treat these as 'starter' questions during the interviews, as part of a semi-directed format, with open-ended questions giving the opportunity to explore any issues or topics that arise. This allows the interviews to range widely over any issues of relevance to staff, ensuring that a complete picture is built up.

Rigid interview formats should be avoided, as these will miss opportunities to identify unexpected issues or needs. Instead, go into the interviews with an unchecked level of curiosity, aiming to uncover how the organisational really works.

4. Stakeholder interviews

A variation on staff interviews, stakeholder sessions focus on middle and senior managers. The goal of these sessions is to understand business drivers and strategic goals, as well as business-area considerations relating to the intranet.

As such, they don't address day-to-day activities and tasks, instead exploring higher-level issues and directions. These sessions will also help to address any internal political requirement to consult with key stakeholder groups.

Available time with senior managers will be limited, so interview sessions may only be 30–45 minutes in length. Use this time to uncover business strategies which can be used as 'hooks' for intranet goals and planning.

5. Workplace observation

Workplace observation involves going 'out into the field' to observe the activities of staff, and the environments in which they work. At it's simplest, it's about watching and listening passively, observing common activities and behaviours.

Workplace observation is particularly effective in environments such as call centres, manufacturing areas, field working, or with on-the-road staff.

This technique is less appropriate in environments where activities cannot be easily seen or heard. For example, staff working in head office would spend the majority of their time in Word or dealing with email, not interesting activities to observe!

Workplace observation is particularly effective at uncovering information on:

- common tasks

- interaction and communication

- working environments

- non-electronic sources of information

- technologies in use

How many staff to involve?

A large organisation may have thousands or tens of thousands of staff. This is a daunting number, and it is clearly not possible to talk to every staff member. Thankfully this is not required.

The fundamental purpose of the research is to identify problems that can be fixed, or opportunities for improvement. The goal is not to find all the issues, as this would be too many to deal with!

Instead, the research focuses on uncovering the biggest or most important issues, or the issues that can be most effectively addressed by the intranet. This greatly cuts down the scope of the research, and eliminates the need for it to be statistically significant.

The general principle is that the needs analysis should continue until nothing sufficiently new is being identified.

In practice, this point is usually reached a lot more quickly than may be expected. In many cases, 3–5 days of needs analysis is enough to gather a substantial volume of information.

Changes to the intranet will also be implemented incrementally. The initial task is therefore to identify improvements that can be conducted over a 6–9 month period.

Once these changes have been made, additional requirements gathering can then be conducted. This is often targeted research that looks at the needs of specific groups, once broader issues with the intranet have been resolved.

Uncovering results and recommendations

Once the research has been completed, the wealth of information needs to be distilled into key findings and recommended actions. In general terms, the process involves examining the observations and discussions across all staff involved, looking for patterns.

When analysing the results, the intranet team is looking for:

- main information sources and key information needs

- major issues impacting on staff's ability to do their jobs

- cultural or organisational issues impacting on the intranet

- key business processes requiring information support

- opportunities for improving information management or delivery

- frustrating business tasks or processes

Based on these findings, a range of strategic (longer-term) and tactical (shorter-term) recommendations can be made about the intranet. These will cover many aspect of intranet design and management.

In most cases, the solutions are obvious, once the problem has been clearly identified. In other cases, further research or planning may be required to determine suitable approaches.

Even a little counts

Intranet teams have limited time, and may struggle to conduct a large-scale piece of intranet research and requirements gathering. It can be effective to bring in outside experts to help with this work, as they bring both a strong set of research skills and a fresh perspective on the organisation.

Even then, budgets may be a limiting factor. Intranet teams should not despair! Even a small amount of research is hugely better than none at all.

Teams can take many opportunities to uncover information about staff needs, including chatting over coffee, dropping into the frontline environment after a meeting, staying a little longer at a regional office during a trip.

Staff will be more than happy to share insights into their work, environment, tasks and frustrations. Over time, the team can pull together these small pieces of information into a clear overall picture that informs intranet improvements.

Understanding staff needs is a life-long task for intranet teams, and it is also one of the most interesting things the team can do. So get out from behind the desk, and discover a hundred new ideas!

Creating intranet personas

This is Owen the Environment Officer. He is an example of an intranet 'persona', an archetypal user of an intranet or website that represents the needs of a larger group of users. Personas act as 'stand-ins' for real users and help guide decisions about intranet functionality and design.

Personas are an effective way of capturing and communicating the results of staff research, and are most suited to front-line and operational roles.

In this case, Owen was created by the Environment Agency in the UK, as part of a major intranet redevelopment. Their personas pack won a Gold Award in the 2007 Intranet Innovation Awards, and three of the personas focused specifically on the intranet: Nikki the New Starter, Owen the Environment Officer and Marcia the Manager.

The personas were created to help authors in the organisation gain a better understanding of their audiences, and therefore assist them to publish better content. They have also helped to build support with senior managers and stakeholders. For more on personas:

www.steptwo.com.au/papers/kmc_personas/

How much do you know about staff needs?

Don't ask staff what they want

Avoid simply asking the question: 'What do you want?' Staff don't know much about intranets, and don't need to (that's our job). These questions can also generate a huge wish-list, without necessarily identifying the key issues and needs.

Use structured research techniques

Use a mix of practical techniques to build a very clear picture of staff needs and issues. These include staff and stakeholder interviews, focus groups and workplace observation. Look for patterns to uncover the biggest issues and to target intranet activities.

Get out into the field

It is incredibly rewarding to spend time with staff who do the actual work, and it will remind you of what the intranet is all about, as well as uncovering hundreds of new ideas.

How to design the intranet

Intranets have a clear goal: to help staff do their jobs. This means ensuring that they can quickly find the information they need, and helping them to confidently complete their tasks online.

In practice, intranets compete against every other way of completing a task, including talking to the person in the next cubicle, picking up the phone, or finding a piece of paper.

Staff can't be forced to use the intranet, and it doesn't make sense to try. Instead, the intranet must be genuinely quicker and easier than other ways of doing things.

Good intranet design recognises and meets these needs. If staff can confidently find what they need, they will naturally use the site.

This is not always easy to achieve, and intranet teams are confronted with many questions:

- What should go on the intranet home page?

- What should the top level navigation items be?

- How do we make sure everything can be found?

- How should intranet pages be laid out?

There are many opinions swirling around intranets, from stakeholders, senior managers, staff and outside experts. These can be challenging to cut through, and the needs of the end user can all too easily be lost in the process.

By taking a structured approach to the design of intranets, teams can confidently deliver a site that works well for staff. Testing with staff uncovers points of pain, provides evidence to back up decisions, and results in a site that matches common usage patterns.

Why staff visit the intranet

There are two fundamental reasons why staff visit the intranet:

- *To find a specific piece of information.* The staff member is looking for a specific fact, detail or figure, such as how much leave they have left to take this year).

- *To complete a specific task.* The staff member has a particular activity to complete that the intranet can help with, such as booking travel or applying for leave.

In both cases, the staff member is not looking for the HR manual, a procedure, or some other general resource. Instead, they are seeking something very specific to meet an immediate need.

It is also important to recognise why staff aren't coming to the intranet. They are not visiting the intranet to just check whether there is updated news, or to browse around to 'find out what's there'. On the whole, staff are also not coming to the intranet for fun. While 'buy and swap' areas are popular, staff almost certainly prefer to have fun in their personal lives rather than on the intranet at work.

When they do open the intranet, staff single-mindedly focus on their task at hand, using navigation or search to get what they need. Once they have completed the task, there is every chance that they close the intranet and return to their normal work.

Staff don't live in the intranet, and their day-to-day work lies in the real world. The intranet is therefore only used when needed, and left to one side the rest of the time.

This is not a problem. As highlighted earlier, the intranet will be used when it is useful. The key is to make the intranet remarkably good at helping staff do what they need to do, and usage will follow.

Help staff complete tasks

As indicated earlier, staff come to an intranet with a particular task in mind, and look for content and functionality that will help them to complete that task. This could be as simple as finding the phone number of a colleague, or as complex as researching, completing and submitting next year's budgets.

The value of an intranet therefore lies in how well it supports common and critical tasks, with successful task support achieved through a combination of:

* providing the right content and functionality

* authoring content so it answers common staff questions and can be easily scanned

* designing the site structure so content and functionality can be found

* providing clear links between content needed to support different aspects of the task

Intranets do not need to be 'sticky', 'engaging' or 'interesting'. They must be useful. When designing or redesigning the intranet, identify the most common (and the most important) tasks that staff have to complete, and ensure that improvements are delivered in these areas.

This principle helps to design every level of the intranet. The home page of the site needs to find a balance between news and links to key content and applications.

The entry page of the HR section should provide direct links to key forms and policies, and not just 'about us' information. Focus on task completion when working on every corner of the site.

Beware of opinions

There is no shortage of opinions on what should go in the intranet, and how it should be designed. These come from stakeholders, senior managers, staff and peers. One of the most difficult aspects of designing an intranet is to cut through these often competing opinions to produce an intranet that works well for staff.

Stakeholders are clearly an important group when designing an intranet, and projects can tend to rely on workshops and sessions with these managers when determining intranet strategies.

There are, however, considerable risks with this 'design by stakeholder' approach. First and foremost, they are not the actual users of the site. It can also lead to a publisher-centric approach to site design, driven by the needs of those who write the content, rather than those who use it.

Once an initial design or prototype has been developed, this is often taken to staff, who are asked 'what do you think of this?' A wide range of staff are involved, each expressing their personal opinion about the relative merits of different options, and making suggestions on potential improvements.

Staff know an awful lot about the work that they do, but they don't know a lot about intranets (nor do they need to!). While their input is valuable, it doesn't necessarily match what they do in practice.

This doesn't mean that stakeholders should be shunned and staff ignored, quite the opposite. What is needed, however, is a structured way of engaging with the organisation that obtains the necessary involvement (and engagement), while confidently producing a site that allows staff to easily find information and complete tasks.

Designing the intranet

The key to making confident progress on an intranet design or redesign is to follow a structured approach. Each step answers fundamental questions, which then provide input into the next steps.

At the broadest level, the following approach should be taken:

1. *Understand staff needs.* Conduct thorough research (as described on page 40) to identify gaps and opportunities. This will also uncover where the current site is working poorly, and where improvements are most needed.

2. *Determine the project scope.* What will be done to the site? What is out of scope? What other improvements will be made? Based on the outcomes of the needs analysis, determine exactly what will be done in the project, using an approach such as the '6x2 methodology' (described on page 90).

3. *Conduct a best-practice redesign.* Restructure the site using practical techniques drawn from the fields of usability and information architecture (described over the page). This best-practice methodology ensures the new site is quick and easy to use.

4. *Migrate content and launch.* Transfer the existing content into the new structure, cleaning up and pruning as you go. Once complete, launch and promote the new site.

Out of this approach will fall a high-level structure for the site, and the design of key pages. It will answer what goes on the home page, and what navigation will be provided.

When done well, this approach will cut through conflicting priorities, and manage the many opinions swirling around the project, to deliver a site that really does work well for staff.

Usability and information architecture

There are two fields of practice which provide a toolbox of practical, research-based techniques for designing sites: usability and information architecture. Together, these give intranet teams a well-tested approach for designing sites that work.

Usability outlines a set of principles and approaches for ensuring that a site is easy to use. The main technique is usability testing, in which staff attempt real-life tasks on the intranet while being observed. The observers don't tell the usability test participant how to use the system and don't answer questions. It is as if the participant were doing the tasks alone.

The usability test identifies the key usability problems with a site, which enables them to be fixed. This can be done early in the project on prototypes, as well as later in the project on draft intranet sites.

Information architecture (IA) encompasses the structure and navigation of the site, and there are a number of practical techniques that can be used to get these right. These include card sorting, which helps the team understand how staff think about information, as well card-based classification evaluation which allows the structure of the site to be tested.

Read the following articles find out more about usability and IA:

- What is usability?
  www.steptwo.com.au/papers/kmc_whatisusability/
- What is information architecture?
  www.steptwo.com.au/papers/kmc_whatisinfoarch/

The book "Don't Make Me Think" by Steve Krug is also highly recommended for all intranet teams.

Best-practice design methodology

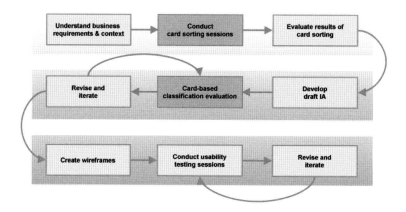

There is a well-tested methodology used by organisations and consulting firms the world over when designing intranets or websites:

1. Understand business requirements and context by conducting research with staff across the organisation.

2. Conduct card sorting to uncover information about how staff think about the information on the intranet.

3. The results of the card sorting are evaluated, and combined with the results of the user research and other sources, to develop a draft site structure.

4. Use card-based classification evaluation to test and revise the structures.

5. Page layouts ('wireframes') are created and then assessed via usability testing with end users.

(For more on these techniques, follow the links on the previous page.)

What every intranet team should know

Intranet Roadmap

There is a lot involved in redesigning an intranet, and the challenge is to keep on top of all of the activities.

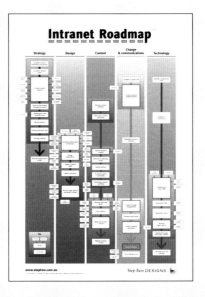

The Intranet Roadmap outlines all the activities needed to design or redesign an intranet. It provides a clear project management methodology and checklist for teams approaching this sometimes daunting task.

Beyond just implementing software or redesigning the site, the Intranet Roadmap covers activities in five key streams:

- strategy
- design
- content
- change & communications
- technology

The Intranet Roadmap is provided as an A1 sized wallchart with supporting booklet, and it adorns the walls of over 500 intranet teams world wide.

For more information or to purchase online: www.steptwo.com.au/products/roadmap

The intranet home page

The intranet home page is the 'front door' to the site, and the most visible element of the site. It can also be the most hotly contested page on the site, with many business areas jostling for space.

Designing a home page is not easy, but the structured approach outlined earlier will greatly help. The starting point is to examine the purpose of the home page, and how this aligns with the needs of staff.

There are three key purposes of every intranet home page:

- news

- navigation (including search)

- access to key tools

Most home pages devote the majority of space to news, with navigation squeezed into the edges. And yet news is not what brings staff to the intranet, it's the need to complete tasks.

We can therefore see that navigation and access to key tools are the most important element of the home page, and space should be devoted accordingly. This includes allocating space within the body of the page to navigation, and not just links across the top of the page, or on the side.

By following a user-centred design methodology, intranet teams can confidently identify the key tasks that the home page should help with, as well as testing draft designs to make sure they work well.

In this way, a home page can be relaunched that is not just refreshed in design, but also dramatically more effective at getting staff to the information and tools they need.

Personalisation

In any large organisation there will be many different staff groups, each with specific intranet requirements, and it is challenging to meet all these needs with a single, static intranet.

The long term goal must be to better target intranets to meet the needs of key staff groups, and 'personalisation' is one potential way of achieving this. This can be split into two separate concepts:

- *User-driven personalisation*, where staff are given the ability to tailor their own experience, such as selecting what elements are displayed on the intranet's home page.

- *Staff segmentation*, where organisations tailor or selectively deliver information or tools to specific audience groups, based on behind-the-scenes knowledge about staff needs.

Of these, the first is the most attractive from a design perspective, as it provides an easy mechanism to build a single 'base' intranet and then to allow staff to configure it as required.

Unfortunately, experience has shown that only 5–10% of staff will make use of these features. While this may change over time, this severely limits the value of personalisation in the short term.

Doing the work on behalf of staff, segmentation provides a very effective way of targeting information delivery. It does, however, require a significant up-front investment in researching staff needs, and ongoing work to ensure that the right information is delivered to each group.

In practice, intranet teams should take an incremental approach to either strategy, recognising that there is no silver bullet that will meet all staff needs without additional effort and careful design.

Ensure the intranet is attractive

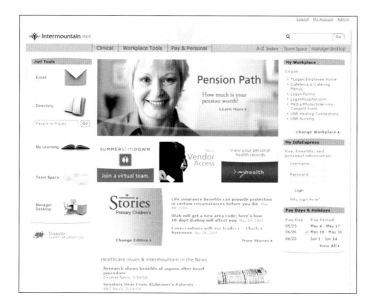

This is the intranet home page at Intermountain Healthcare, a community-owned healthcare provider in Utah and Idaho. It presents a clean, modern professional image that says: 'This is an intranet we care enough about to do well'.

Intranets don't need to be 'sexy', but they do need to have a strong visual design (and this should be different to the public website). They cannot afford to be ugly, poorly designed or dated in appearance.

A polished and well-designed appearance shows (at least in part) that the organisation is prepared to devote resources to the intranet, and that it is an important platform. At the most basic level, good design has an emotional impact, and this should not be ignored for intranets.

Is your intranet easy and effective to use?

Intranets must work well for staff

There is no way to trick staff into visiting the intranet, or forcing them to use it. Instead, the intranet must offer the simplest and easiest way for staff to find information and complete tasks. (News and social elements are not enough to regularly draw staff to the intranet.)

Follow a best-practice design methodology

Intranets are flooded with opinions from staff and stakeholders, but these don't help to design an intranet that really works well. Instead, follow a structured methodology that provides practical techniques for designing and testing the site.

There is no one 'perfect' design

There are many ways of designing an intranet, and the best is the one that fits the organisation's specific needs and practices. Follow a structured approach to the design process, and the result will be an intranet that you are confident works well.

How to deliver great content

One of the primary purposes of an intranet is to provide a home for corporate and business unit content. To be of real use, however, this must be good content, not just poorly written materials brought together in a single location.

When we say 'good content', we mean content that is:

- useful

- accurate

- complete

- up to date

- trustworthy

- easy to read

- concise

- targeted to audience needs

- delivered in a suitable format

- cross-linked

The intranet can easily grow to thousands or tens of thousands of pages of content, with a similar number of linked documents. These pages may be maintained by dozens or hundreds of authors scattered across the organisation.

Delivering consistently good content across the whole intranet is no easy task, and there is not a silver bullet strategy that will guarantee content quality.

There are, however, a number of practical approaches that can be taken to steadily improve, and then maintain, content quality.

Not all content needs to be of equal quality

The first thing to recognise is that not all content needs to be of equal quality. Content published to the intranet varies greatly, in both importance and target audience.

Some information is central to the organisation, and the intranet. This includes key resources for staff and core corporate information, such as:

- corporate policies and procedures

- front-line support materials (such as in call centres)

- corporate communications

Used by the entire organisation, these materials must be very accurate, carefully written and well structured. They must also be kept up to date, in sync with underlying organisational or legislative changes.

Beyond core corporate information, intranets contain a wide variety of material that does not need to meet the same exacting quality standards.

At the other extreme, items of content such as project updates or meeting minutes are only needed by a small audience, and are intended to reflect changes or decisions, rather than corporate policies. It is more important to have this kind of information published quickly than to try to make sure it is perfectly written and presented.

Specialist or technical content will have a very small audience, or may only be used within a single area of the organisation. Again, it is less important that this kind of material is fully polished to perfection before publishing.

Target efforts to highest value content

Many intranet teams strive to publish 'perfect' content across their whole sites. While this is a natural goal, it is unrealistic, and it often leads to burnt-out intranet teams.

Intranet teams have limited time and resources. In some organisations there may only be a handful of staff, responsible for managing an intranet consisting of tens of thousands of pages. Similar challenges exist for authors and publishers in business units.

A pragmatic approach needs to be taken, targeting efforts at the highest value content, and applying progressively looser standards to the rest of the site. This ensures that the most important or most frequently-used content meets the highest standards.

Taking this approach is not admitting defeat. Instead, it is about ensuring that the intranet is maximally useful, recognising that content quality is only one element of this.

Intranet teams also have more strategic responsibilities than ensuring correct spelling on all pages, or ensuring that punctuation is used correctly. Time must be set aside for these bigger tasks, to ensure that the intranet is steadily improving over time.

When evaluating the possible publishing models that can be used on an intranet, recognise that many of them require considerable ongoing effort by both the decentralised authors and central teams. Use the more formal publishing methods sparingly, and target them to the highest value content.

Define and formalise multiple levels of quality across the intranet. Develop appropriate policies and standards to match, and communicate these to intranet authors and content owners.

Use a mix of publishing models

There are many ways of publishing and managing content on an intranet, ranging from fully centralised to completely decentralised, and everything in between.

The approaches taken in organisations can be grouped into five broad categories:

1. *Fully centralised publishing.* All content is published by the central intranet team, with business areas contributing information via email, Word documents and other source documents.

2. *Decentralised publishing.* Business areas are responsible for publishing and managing their own content. Authors in each business area can publish directly to the intranet.

3. *Publishing with review.* Content is produced by authors within business areas, but goes through some form of review before it is published to the intranet, such as being checked by a manager or being reviewed by the central team.

4. *Federated publishing.* A hybrid model is followed, with each business area appointing a coordinator who takes responsibility for managing intranet authors within their area. This devolves the review process to each business area.

5. *End-user content contribution.* Staff across the organisation can contribute news items or content to the site directly, without having a formal role as an 'author'. This could involve allowing staff to directly publish news items or calendar events, or the use of wikis and blogs.

There is no single best publishing approach, and each has its strengths and weaknesses.

Pick the right models

With the diversity of approaches to intranet publishing, it is important to pick the right mix of models to match the organisation's culture and needs.

Target the approaches to fit the skills of the authors, the nature of the content, the section of the site, and the need for content quality.

Elements from each of the basic models outlined above can also be combined into dozens of different hybrid approaches. Don't be afraid to experiment, and to work with authors to identify new approaches.

Recognise that more robust models require greater time and effort, and these should be targeted to the most important content. Lower value content can be directly published, or managed more lightly. (Less is more!)

Within business areas there will be staff who have been assigned the job of intranet author without a background in writing or the web. These less experienced authors will require greater support, up to and including publishing content on their behalf. Smaller business areas may also require greater support.

Publishing approaches should also be adjusted over time to reflect changing circumstances. For example, centralised publishing may be used for a smaller business unit until they can obtain further resources, when a switch is made to a federated model. A review process can also be used to provide feedback to novice authors, who are then switched to direct publishing once their knowledge grows.

The key to intranet publishing success is to get the right mix of flexibility and formal processes, and the right balance between high quality content and streamlined publishing approaches.

Focus on the people aspects

A fundamental rule is this: the right content is produced if the right people are doing the right things. These are people issues. Recognising this, intranet teams should focus their efforts on the people involved in the site, authors in particular:

- *Understand the motivations of authors.* In order to help authors in business areas, central teams need to understand their skills, motivations and objectives.

- *Help authors to be effective.* The greater the skills and knowledge of authors, the better the content that will be produced. With many authors lacking in-depth publishing experience, this support becomes doubly important (and effective).

- *Build bridges between authors and the central intranet team.* The intranet team cannot afford to have an adversarial relationship with business areas or decentralised authors. Good relations should therefore be built, sustained and grown.

- *Encourage good practices rather then enforcement.* Authors don't report to the intranet team, and the central team has no formal way of enforcing policies or procedures. 'Soft' approaches should therefore be used wherever possible, with the aim of encouraging good practices.

- *Present a human face.* Communications are more effective when they are done face-to-face. Ensure that the intranet team deals in person with business areas and authors.

Intranet teams deliver great content across the site by working effectively with staff and stakeholders, understanding internal politics, and communicating well.

The limits of workflow

Most publishing systems, such as content management systems (CMS) and portals, contain 'workflow' capabilities which can be used to automate the management of content reviews.

These establish a sequence of steps that content must go through, between the author and the final site. For example, content could be reviewed by the local manager, checked by legal, and double-checked by the central intranet team. The goal is to bring greater control to the publishing process, as well as improving content quality.

Workflow is most effective when there are clearly-defined, well-understood business processes already in place. The workflow rules can then be set up to match these existing processes. An example would be automating the review and publication of a standard report every month.

Simple workflow can also be useful, with one or two steps between the author and the published page on the intranet. Beyond this, however, workflow can prove to be ineffective or even problematic.

Organisations are complex. In practice, the 'rules' that determine who should review and approve a piece of content depend on many factors, including: type of content, subject, author, area of the business, potential legal exposure, publishing time frame, and more.

While the goal may be to implement a few 'standard' workflow rules, these generally fail to address the complexity that exists within organisations. In some cases, workflow is bypassed by the majority of authors, in the interests of easy or timely publishing. In this situation, the workflow isn't really put into practice at all.

Realistic expectations must be set for the use of workflow, as it is supported in current publishing tools. In practice, most authors should be able to publish content directly to the intranet, with only more important content being managed through the use of automated workflow.

Pursue multiple approaches

In addition to establishing suitable publishing processes, there are a range of supporting strategies and approaches that can be explored:

- *Create standards and guidelines.* A set of intranet governance documents provides a range of information for authors and site managers, with the goal of increasing consistency and quality across the whole intranet.

- *Provide author training, mentoring and support.* Building the skills and knowledge of authors is vital in a decentralised model, including formalised training and documentation and ongoing mentoring.

- *Implement review and expiry dates.* Most content management systems will provide automated dates to remind authors to review content, and to take it off the site when it has expired.

- *Conduct projects to improve key areas.* Some areas of the intranet will be more important than others and there is value in devoting central resources to improving some of these key areas, such as HR, finance and IT.

- *Establish intranet feedback mechanisms.* Implement a simple system that staff can use to provide feedback on the intranet, offering them a single point of contact to report missing or incorrect information, or to ask questions.

These are just a few of the approaches that can be taken. Step Two has published a mammoth mindmap containing hundreds of ideas, and this can be downloaded from:

www.steptwo.com.au/columntwo/files/intranetcontent_mindmap.pdf

Establish an authoring community

In addition to the approaches outlined above, consider establishing a 'community of practice' for intranet authors. These bring together everyone involved in creating, publishing and maintaining content, including:

- authors

- publishers

- reviewers

- central intranet team

The community meets regularly, ideally face-to-face on a monthly or bi-monthly basis. If this is impractical, physical sessions can be support by online collaboration, phone or video conferencing.

The goal is to establish a vibrant, active community that has a clear purpose for both participants and the organisation as a whole.

Group dynamics makes these gatherings work. Trust is built up in person, while peer pressure and other social factors can help to bring everyone together. The group then benefits from the input of many, rather than just the directions set in place by the central team.

The community should quickly build a shared sense of ownership amongst intranet stakeholders, as well as providing an effective forum for group training and the establishment of appropriate governance. This reduces the amount of work required from the intranet team, while improving the support for authors.

In our experience, establishing this kind of authoring community is the single most effective way of improving content in a decentralised publishing environment.

Deliver content that works for staff and the organisation

Focus on the right content

Not all content needs to be of equal quality, with core corporate information rating much higher than material to be read by just a handful of staff. Target your limited resources and time to the highest value content.

Establish a mix of publishing models

There are many ways of managing the publishing process, each with its strengths and weaknesses. Establish the right mix of centralised, decentralised, reviewed and user-generated publishing.

Manage content on many fronts

There is no silver bullet that delivers great content. Explore a range of approaches for building author skills, establishing appropriate governance, and closing the feedback loop. Adapt over time to fit changing circumstances and needs.

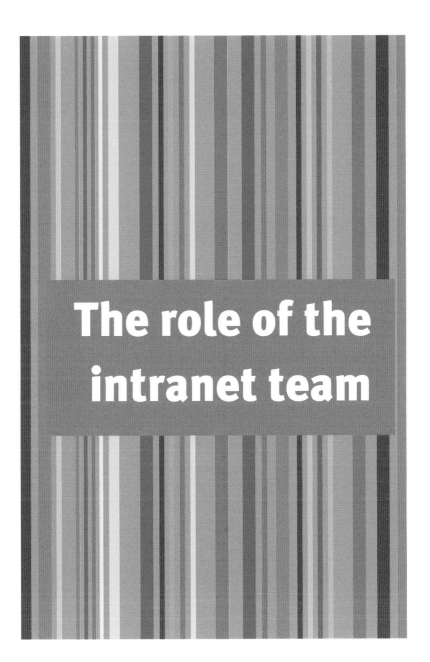

The role of the intranet team

Intranets don't run themselves. Even in a decentralised model, there needs to be a strong central intranet team who take responsibility for activities such as:

- managing the intranet home page

- structuring the top levels of the site

- promoting the use of the site

- determining an overall intranet strategy

- establishing policies and governance

- reviewing pages published by business areas

- supporting intranet authors and publishers

- liaising with intranet stakeholders

- managing key technologies, such as the CMS and search engine

- conducting intranet improvement projects

In any organisation over a few hundred staff, there should be someone with clearly defined responsibility for managing the intranet. Larger organisations require a full-time team of at least two people, probably more.

This still leaves many questions: who should own the intranet? where should the intranet team sit? what should they be doing with their time, and how can they be successful?

If there has been confusion about the role of intranets within organisations, this is doubly true for intranet teams. While there is no single answer for some of these questions, there are a number of strategies that can be applied to achieve a successful intranet (and a happy intranet team).

What every intranet team should know

There is no shortage of work to be done by the central intranet team

Who should own the intranet?

The starting point to successful intranet management is to determine who should be the overall owner of the site, and where the intranet team should be located. By 'owner', we mean the person or team responsible for making overall decisions about the intranet, developing strategies, and working with other intranet stakeholders.

While the responsibility for driving the intranet must be given to a single business area, this group must be located within the right area of the organisation if the intranet is to succeed. Without a strong team to drive the intranet, the site will struggle to prosper and grow.

There are some obvious organisational areas who could own and manage the intranet:

- communications

- IT

- human resources

- knowledge or information management

Each area brings its specific area of expertise, matching up to the four purposes outlined earlier. Outside their core focus, however, each group is likely to have a number of weaknesses.

For example, if the intranet is run by the communications team, there will typically be a strong focus on using the intranet as a communications platform. Similarly, intranet teams located within KM or library sections tend to emphasise the role of the intranet as a corporate repository of information, or as a knowledge-sharing platform.

IT focuses on application development and the management of the technical platform, and often devolves ownership of content and communication, along with broader intranet strategy, 'out to the business'.

At the end of the day, it doesn't matter who owns the intranet, as long as they have the right skills and focus. They also need to have strong support from their direct management, and sufficient resources.

Experience has shown that successful intranet teams have:

- a genuine interest in meeting staff (and business) needs

- strong people and communications skills

- sufficient time to devote to continuously driving the intranet forward

- excellent support from a senior sponsor

Depending on the organisational structure and culture, this focus could be found within any of the groups listed above. While a single owner must be identified, no single group will have the required skills and resources to fully deliver the intranet.

In practice, effort will be required from IT, communications, HR and other stakeholder groups. For this reason, a broader governance model must be established that allows all of these groups to participate in the maintenance and development of the intranet.

Covering all bases

While it is human nature for intranet teams to focus on the areas that they have the strongest background in, the site as a whole will not succeed if the other aspects are neglected.

In all too many situations the intranet team will state that 'applications are outside their scope' or that 'news is the responsibility of the communications team'.

While the intranet team will always need to work closely with other business areas to deliver the intranet, they must also have a clear and coherent vision for the site as a whole.

Without this single direction, problems commonly arise, such as applications being managed completely separately from the policies they relate to.

Only when there is one group coordinating and guiding all four intranet purposes does it become possible to deliver a site that meets the needs of the whole organisation. This means that intranet teams need to take on responsibility for the whole intranet, or pass it across to someone else.

Spending team time

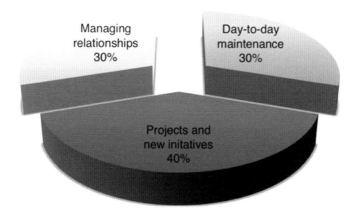

Intranet teams need to use their time wisely. It is very easy to fall into the trap of dealing with urgent requests and problems, and never actually make any longer-term progress.

Effective intranet teams must plan how they will deliver both short-term and long-term benefits to their organisations.

The rule of thumb for intranet resources is:

- 30% effort for day-to-day maintenance

- 40% effort for projects and new initiatives

- 30% effort managing relationships with staff and stakeholders

For a team of one this can mean carefully dividing up the work week into different activities. In a larger team, these responsibilities can be split between different roles.

What every intranet team should know

Day-to-day maintenance can include publishing and maintaining content, providing support for publishers, fixing technical problems, maintaining the home page and reviewing content areas with owners.

If day-to-day maintenance of the intranet absorbs excessive amounts of the team's time the intranet will never progress. This can lead to the the team becoming disengaged and experiencing a never-ending workload.

Projects and new initiatives can include adding a new content area to the intranet, redesigning the site, implementing a new content management system, incorporating collaboration tools, improving search results, or a hundred other improvements.

Projects are where intranet teams build the most credibility. Each time the intranet is improved teams must ensure there are tangible and visible benefits. All changes must be managed, communicated and celebrated.

Good relationships underpin every successful intranet. The intranet team is the often the 'enabler' with the expert knowledge to manage the intranet and bring it all together. However this cannot be done without building partnerships with other areas of the business.

Relationships also provide the opportunity to identify opportunities where the intranet can support business initiatives.

The key to these relationships is to understand what staff need, how the organisation works and what is currently important to the organisation.

Relationships are two-way connections between the team and others. Spending time building and sustaining relationships will help the intranet team to be effective, and to complete key projects with the support of the organisation.

Playing a leadership role

All too often, centralised intranet teams find themselves battling with decentralised authors to enforce consistency and quality standards.

Not only is this fighting ultimately fruitless, it can be very damaging for the morale of all participants, and potentially crippling for the future of the intranet itself.

In these situations, intranet teams need to find a new approach, and new ways of working with their decentralised authors. The first step is to lose the language of enforcement.

Intranet teams should ban the use of the following terms (among others):

- enforcement

- compliance

- audits

- standards

- policies

- regulations

- obligations

- force

- require

This is not to say that standards and governance are abandoned, but it does mean that intranet teams should make a conscious effort to use the 'carrot' rather than the 'stick' when dealing with stakeholders.

The carrot is almost always better than the stick

Fundamentally, no-one reports to the intranet team, making it difficult for the team to enforce standards or demand compliance.

Intranet teams should instead take on a leadership, coaching and influencing role in the organisation. Effective leadership is all about creating a shared vision, and making it a reality.

Coaching is the process of working with people to help them achieve their goals. As discussed earlier, this involves building relationships instead of relying on enforcement and compliance.

Looking across many organisations, the most successful intranet teams are 'people people', strong in communication and relationship building, more than just having specialist or technical skills. Successful intranets are about making friends and influencing people.

Who owns and runs your intranet?

Identify a clear intranet owner

There are many potential owners of the intranet, including IT and communications. At the end of the day, it doesn't matter who manages the site, as long as they have the right skills and focus, and the support of their management. They also need to accept responsibility for creating a vision that encompasses all four intranet purposes.

Spend your time wisely

It is easy to become overwhelmed with day-to-day maintenance of the site, but teams should spend only 30% of their time on this. 40% of the team's time should be devoted to projects and new initiatives, while 30% should be allocated to managing relationships.

Build relationships and influence

Intranet teams can make progress by simply banning words such as 'compliance', 'enforcement' and 'auditing'. Recognising that no-one directly reports to the intranet team, the team should instead build relationships and a shared vision.

How to plan intranet improvements

There is no shortage of improvements that can be made to an intranet, from minor fixes to major redevelopments. We have often noted that many intranet problems are the accumulation of many smaller issues, such as:

- the 'A-Z of policies' page, with many policies under the letter 'T' (for 'the policy on…')

- the 'useful tools' page, packed with confusing acronyms

- the home page of HR filled with 'about us' information

- confusing navigation in the IT section

Beyond this, there can often be bigger problems, including the overall structure of the intranet, ineffective search, and dated designs.

These are just the issues to be resolved. There are also a hundred potential improvements, including new functionality and tools. The typical intranet team has a wish list of activities a mile long.

The challenge is finding the time and resources to get this work done. There are many demands on the time of the intranet team, including day-to-day maintenance.

In addition to ensuring that sufficient time is allocated to improvements (see page 84), intranet teams also benefit from having a disciplined approach to planning and prioritising projects.

The '6x2 methodology' for intranets provides a simple methodology for intranet planning, that focuses on delivering high-impact improvements in the short term, while working towards longer term goals. By factoring in constraints, this methodology also gives intranet teams the confidence that activities really can be completed, even in a continually changing environment.

What every intranet team should know

Beware of the 'big bang' project

There are some intranet projects that inevitably become very large undertakings. Conducting a complete intranet redesign is one such project. Once all the elements have been considered, this will take at least 12–18 months.

Considerable expectation rests on these projects: they must fix every intranet issue, and deliver every desired feature. This is on top of moving to a new technology platform, restructuring the site, and migrating all the content.

Inevitably, limited resources and other constraints start to impact on these projects. Time starts to run out, and the effort of managing the technology and content migration limits how many improvements can be made.

The result is an intranet that is somewhat better than the old one, but by no means perfect. The intranet team is exhausted, as are the content authors and owners. A significant budget has been spent, and the organisation isn't in a hurry to allocate more.

This is a perfect description of the era of repeated redesigns, as outlined on page 13. The intranet changes, but what is delivered is not necessarily very different from the previous site.

Redesigning the intranet isn't the hardest project, and there can be even more ambitious projects, often relating to organisation-wide changes in work practices or culture. These include rolling out big new document management or knowledge management systems, or encouraging every staff member to use collaboration tools.

These projects are risky: big bang activities that will either succeed dramatically, or fail spectacularly.

Steadily deliver incremental improvements

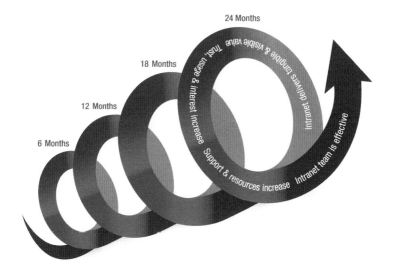

Intranet teams benefit from delivering ongoing incremental improvements, as this helps to build an upwards spiral:

- The intranet team delivers new content and capabilities.

- This enhances levels of trust, usage and interest among staff, content owners and stakeholders.

- Having demonstrated their ability to add value, the intranet team is able to gain some additional support and resources.

- The intranet team is therefore a little more effective, and better-placed, to support the ongoing improvement of the intranet.

At the end of each turn of the spiral, new functionality or content is delivered that helps position the intranet (and the intranet team) for the next round of improvements.

What every intranet team should know

Delivering every six months

As outlined earlier, intranet teams benefit from steadily delivering new functionality and content on the site, and in the process building support for future activities.

Releasing intranet 'upgrades' every six months works well. This is the core of the '6x2 methodology': two six-month periods, the first six months planned and executed in detail, with sketched-out ideas for the second six months. This adds up to 12 months of planning, and becomes the basis for a solid and ongoing intranet strategy.

Six months is not long, deliberately so. The longer the project, the more likely it is that organisational changes (budget, structure, politics, competing projects) will derail the work. Anything less than six months will leave too little time to deliver anything of consequence.

Within the six months, activities are planned that deliver the greatest impact within current constraints. This is achieved through the following steps:

1. uncover and brainstorm potential intranet activities

2. identify criteria for determining which activities to pick

3. identify constraints that limit the intranet and intranet team

4. review each activity in turn against the criteria and constraints

5. determine a draft list of activities for the coming six months

6. assess the list as a whole against the criteria and constraints

7. obtain management signoff and develop a concrete project plan

8. implement and launch the improvements!

Identify criteria

The starting point for intranet planning is to identify the criteria for choosing which activities to conduct in the coming six months. Brainstorm a list of possible criteria, using the following questions to guide the discussions:

- Why choose something for inclusion in the next six months?

- What would make us choose one item instead of another?

The specific criteria will vary depending on the state of the intranet, the organisation's priorities and culture, and the broader intranet strategy. Some sample criteria used by intranet teams:

- increases intranet usage

- helps staff do their jobs

- streamlines business processes

- demonstrates the value of the intranet

- builds momentum for the intranet (and intranet team)

- strategically important

- high visibility and impact

- generates interest and enthusiasm

- saves money

- reduces business risks

Once all the possible criteria have been identified, select the *six most important criteria*, and use these to guide the selection of project activities.

Identify constraints

Once the criteria have been captured, the intranet team identifies the constraints that are restricting their ability to deliver an intranet additions or improvements.

These should not be hard to list, as intranet teams are keenly aware of the limitations and organisational issues that are holding back their longer-term intranet plans.

Some sample constraints:

- staff resources (eg 2 team members)

- budget ($)

- limited IT support

- no executive sponsorship

- low level of engagement from the business

- lack of overall intranet strategy

- duplicated or competing platforms

- lack of content ownership

- business 'silos'

- resistance to change from staff

- not all staff can access the intranet

Once the full list of constraints has been identified, select the *top six constraints* on the intranet (and the intranet team). This will help to focus discussions when evaluating individual ideas and activities.

Ruthlessly assess ideas

The core of the planning methodology is the evaluation of all the possible ideas against both the criteria and the constraints. This ensures that the activities that are chosen are not just doable, but are also worth doing.

Organise a workshop with the whole of the intranet team, and work through each of the possible ideas or activities. Ask two key questions:

- Does this idea match the key criteria?

- Is the idea achievable within the key constraints?

An idea doesn't have to match all of the criteria, but it must fulfil at least a few. Any ideas that don't match any of the criteria are automatically eliminated, without assessing the constraints. When assessing against the constraints, the idea or activity must be achievable in light of all of the constraints.

Based on the results of the assessment against the criteria and constraints, make a decision for each item as follows:

- Yes: the idea meets one or more of the important criteria and is achievable within the constraints.

- No: the idea does not meet any of the important criteria or cannot be achieved given the constraints.

- Maybe: it is not clear whether the idea is achievable and may need to be investigated further. (These must all be converted into a yes or no by the end of the planning process.)

The result is a draft action plan for the coming months. This is a simple planning approach, but is very effective at cutting through assumptions and helping the team to deliver successful projects.

Deliver tangible and visible outcomes

Regardless of the approach taken to planning, intranet teams should be guided by two words:

- Tangible: the intranet team can clearly demonstrate the impact or value of the activity for the organisation.

- Visible: the improvement can be seen or recognised by a large number of staff, ideally the organisation as a whole.

Applying these principles to common activities:

- *Improving search.* Tangible and visible, particularly if there are serious problems with the current search engine.

- *Creating a new call centre solution.* Tangible and visible, as this can have a dramatic impact on customer satisfaction.

- *Implementing a new CMS.* Tangible but not visible, as benefits are only felt by several dozen authors and site administrators.

- *Improving the site structure.* Visible but not necessarily tangible, as changes are seen, but it is hard to explain the effort involved.

- *Improving metadata consistency.* Not tangible or visible, as it is difficult for the intranet team to even explain this activity, let alone to demonstrate the value to the wider organisation.

- *Improving content.* Not strongly tangible or visible, as this is a long-term activity that can be hard to clearly demonstrate.

By focusing on tangible and visible activities, intranet teams build support throughout the organisation, enhancing their credibility and setting the team up for future projects.

6x2 methodology for intranets

There is much more to this planning methodology than can be described in six pages. The *6x2 methodology for intranets* report provides a full walkthrough of the approach, including step-by-step instructions, tips, tricks and samples.

The methodology provides a simple and pragmatic approach that can be used by intranet teams of any size (from one person to a dozen or more). It is equally applicable in private and public organisations, and the more complex and difficult the intranet, the better the approach works.

6x2 methodology for intranets

James Robertson
FEBRUARY 2007

Step Two DESIGNS
www.steptwo.com.au

The 95 page report contains:

* unique methodology for intranet planning
* underlying principles and philosophies
* step-by-step instructions on using the methodology
* detailed examples and guidelines
* case studies of the methodology in practice

Use this report to discover a new way of building a successful intranet (and a happy intranet team).

For more information or to purchase a copy online:
www.steptwo.com.au/products/6x2

What are you launching in the next six months?

Deliver new features every six months

Over time, steadily delivering intranet additions and improvements will lead to a truly great site, more than a single 'big bang' project. Plan six months ahead in detail, and sketch out the six months after that.

Select activities for maximum impact

When planning intranet activities, work within constraints and have a clear set of criteria for selecting improvements. Following a structured planning methodology will help to cut through assumptions to deliver the best possible project plan.

Make sure it's tangible and visible

Worthwhile activities don't count if they aren't noticed or valued by the organisation. Focus on delivering improvements that will build support for the intranet, and position the team for the next round of work.

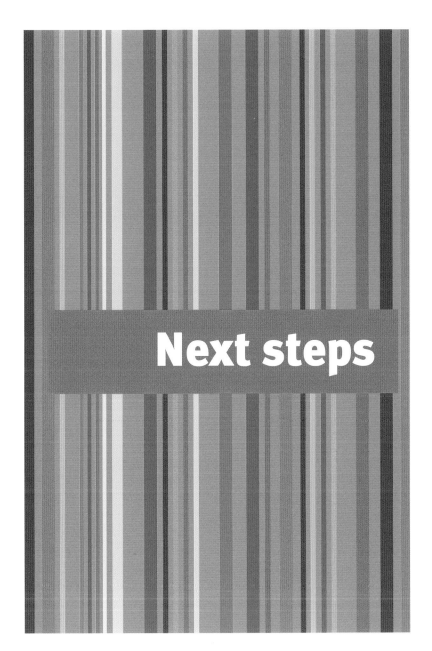

Next steps

Further reading

Step Two is the most prolific publisher of intranet information in the world, including hundreds of articles, plus reports, presentations and videos.

All the resources listed on this page are free, and intranet teams are encouraged to make use of them to support ongoing intranet management and improvement:

- *Articles.* Step Two has published 200+ articles on a wide range of intranet, usability, information architecture and content management topics. These are free on our website:

  www.steptwo.com.au/category/papers/

- *Papers announce list.* Three new articles are published each month, and we provide an announce list to inform you of new articles:

  www.steptwo.com.au//subscribe/

- *Presentations and slidecasts.* Step Two routinely shares the majority of presentations given at local and international events, including a growing a number of slidecasts (slides plus audio). These can be found on Slideshare.

  www.slideshare.net/jamesr/slideshows

- *Videos.* We have recorded a number of video interviews with winners of the Intranet Innovation Awards. Five to six minutes in length, these are designed to generate enthusiasm as well as answering key questions.

  www.youtube.com/user/StepTwoDesigns

Step Two consulting services

Step Two provides vendor-neutral consulting services, and we are one of the few firms to cover all aspects of intranets.

This includes:

- developing an intranet strategy

- redesigning the intranet

- uncovering intranet opportunities

- creating a new intranet

- improving intranet usability

- making the intranet work better

- taking a successful intranet to the next level

- selecting a suitable content management system (CMS)

- improving intranet search

- developing a collaboration strategy

We provide services throughout Australia and New Zealand, and also for select organisations worldwide. We have a long client list, and experience with both public and private sector organisations.

In addition to consulting, we also provide in-house training and mentoring. These are designed to build internal skills, allowing limited resources to be targeted in the most effective way.

For more information on our services, please visit our website: www.steptwo.com.au

intranetleadership**forum**
many ideas. one purpose.

The Intranet Leadership Forum is a unique professional community for intranet managers and teams in Australia. The Forum provides support to intranet teams, and members are connected with other intranet professionals who are tackling similar intranet projects and issues.

Members have access to real-life solutions for their organisation's intranet issues from peers who have already found the answers, saving time and money. Strict confidentiality supports this sharing, and protects insights.

Current members include ANZ, Bureau of Meteorology, Caltex, Commonwealth Bank, Department of Employment and Workplace Relations (DEWR), and NSW Department of Primary Industries.

Key benefits include:

- Three facilitated ½ day workshops with the topics selected by members, providing an opportunity for key challenges and new ideas to be explored.

- Annual two-day intensive workshop that covers the latest techniques and best thinking on intranet strategy and management.

- Members-only website with member profiles and screen shots.

- Members-only email list to allow you to ask questions and obtain assistance on current challenges.

For more information:
www.intranetleadership.com.au

Designing intranets: creating sites that work

The definitive textbook for intranet teams. In 275 pages, this book walks through a practical user-centred approach to the design process, richly illustrating each step with full-colour screenshots from organisations across the globe.

A perfect complement to *What every intranet team should know*.

Almost every medium-to-large organisation has an intranet, yet many staff complain that they can't find what they need to do their jobs.

Designing a successful intranet has been a black art to date, with limited opportunities to see other intranets or to share practical approaches. This has made it hard for intranet and project teams to be confident that they are producing the best possible site.

Thankfully there is now a definitive textbook for teams starting into a design or redesign project. Drawing on more than 10 years industry experience, this book is written by the leaders in intranet thinking.

To obtain a copy:
www.steptwo.com.au/products/designing-intranets

Intranet Innovation Awards

The Intranet Innovation Awards celebrate new ideas and innovative approaches to the enhancement and delivery of intranets.

Uniquely, these awards recognise individual intranet improvements, and not intranets as a whole. The awards are about improving all intranets, by sharing great ideas and increasing the pace of innovation across the whole of the intranet community.

Every idea, no matter how small, adds to our understanding of what it means to have a successful intranet.

With winners across four categories (core functionality, communication and collaboration, frontline delivery and business solutions), there are valuable ideas for every intranet team.

Each year, a report is produced that shares the full results of the awards, including screenshots and details of the winning entries. Commended entries provide further insights and examples.

Use these reports to discover where intranets are innovating, and to find ideas that can be implemented on your intranet.

For more information:
www.steptwo.com.au/iia

Improving Intranet Search

Poor search is one of the greatest sources of user frustration with intranets. Worse yet, the inadequacies of search may be consigning the intranet as a whole to failure.

The problem is that few search solutions have been effectively designed, in terms of the interfaces provided to staff or the behind-the-scenes improvements needed to make search work like magic.

Even just a few days devoted to improving search can have significant impact. If resources are then allocated to steadily maintaining and enhancing search, it will not take long to deliver an extraordinary search solution.

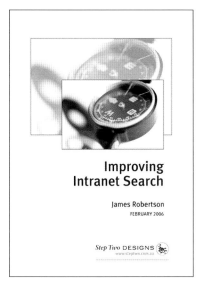

Improving Intranet Search

James Robertson
FEBRUARY 2006

Step Two DESIGNS
www.steptwo.com.au

In this 115-page report you will find key principles of effective search, a nine-step methodology for improving search and practical ideas on how to tune search.

Use this report to make immediate improvements to intranet search, and to then plan a program of work that will deliver a powerful search solution for staff.

For more information:
www.steptwo.com.au/products/search

Staff Directories report

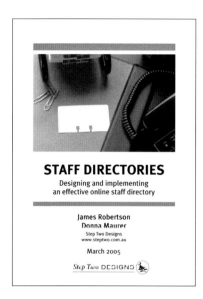

STAFF DIRECTORIES
Designing and implementing
an effective online staff directory

James Robertson
Donna Maurer
Step Two Designs
www.steptwo.com.au

March 2005

Step Two DESIGNS

Also known as phone directories, phone lists and corporate whitepages, staff directories are always the most-used feature of corporate intranets. More than any other tool, they are used every day throughout the organisation.

Staff directories can be much more than just a list of names and phone numbers. They can capture organisational structure, locations, photos, skills and expertise, projects, blogs and much more.

Like any tool, however, staff directories must be carefully designed to be effective and usable. This "better practice" report is designed to capture the experience gained across dozens of organisations to give you clear and practical ideas on how to design, implement and maintain your staff directory

In this 91-page report you will find detailed exploration of staff directory fields, design guidelines for all staff directory pages and tips relating to all aspects of staff directories. The report is also richly illustrated with dozens of screenshots that provide concrete examples of the features and approaches being discussed.

For more information:
www.steptwo.com.au/products/staffdirectories

Governance and support for SharePoint team sites

Microsoft SharePoint is now rapidly spreading through organisations. In terms of team collaboration, this is meeting a very real need, replacing the reliance on email and shared network folders.

If unmanaged, however, this explosive growth will generate more problems than benefits. What is needed is clear governance and support, and this best practice case study shows the way. A must for any organisation planning on deploying SharePoint team sites.

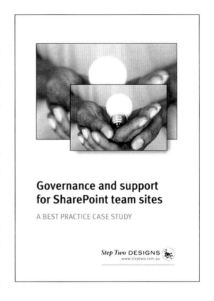

Governance and support for SharePoint team sites

A BEST PRACTICE CASE STUDY

Step Two DESIGNS

This 24-page report features a case study from Transfield Services, a global services firm headquartered in Australia, which won a Gold Award in the 2008 Intranet Innovation Awards.

Transfield's key innovation was productising their approach to collaboration spaces with 'Team Sites in a Box', and compiling a near-perfect design, support and governance methodology and model, which then saw rapid, but controlled uptake within the organisation.

For more information:
www.steptwo.com.au/products/teamsites

Content Management Requirements Toolkit

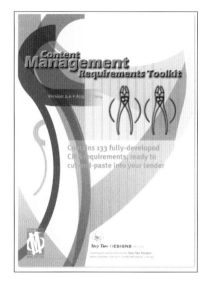

Choosing a content management system (CMS) is not easy. There are hundreds of products in the marketplace, all with highly-variable capabilities. In this rapidly-evolving environment, the challenge is to find the CMS that best matches your business needs.

The Content Management Requirements Toolkit stands as the most comprehensive set of CMS requirements in the industry. Taking a vendor-neutral approach, the Toolkit also provides a comprehensive guide to writing CMS scenarios, as well as a detailed overview of the whole selection process.

This resource lights the way for teams confronted with the sometimes overwhelming task of navigating through the CMS selection process.

The Requirements Toolkit contains 133 fully-developed CMS requirements, across five main categories. These are ready to be cut-and-pasted into your content management tender, saving days of effort and ensuring that nothing is missed.

For more information:
www.steptwo.com.au/products/toolkit

**Art Center College Library
1700 Lida Street
Pasadena, CA 91103**

13. Aug.13   Andrew   22-00   12/611